Polar Be

Contents

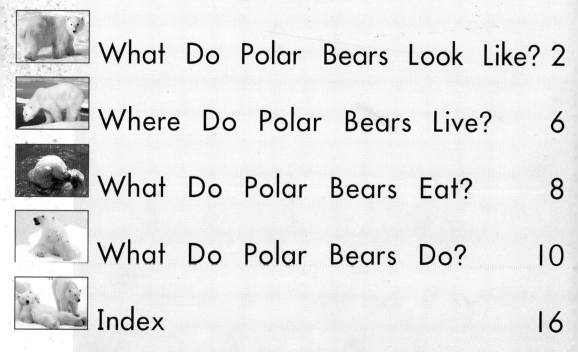

What Do Polar Bears Look Like?

Polar bears are big bears.
They have white fur.
They have small eyes.
They have small ears.
They have sharp claws.

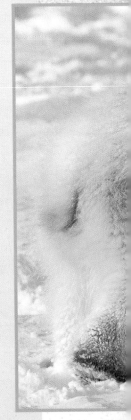

Ear

Eye

Claws

Fur

3

Polar bears
cannot see well.
They cannot hear
well, but they
can smell well.

Where Do Polar Bears Live?

Polar bears live on the ice and snow. They live near the sea.

Arctic Ocean

Greenland

Alaska

Canada

United States

KEY

 Where polar bears live

What Do Polar Bears Eat?

Polar bears eat fish. They eat seals and walruses, too.

8

Salmon

Seal

Walrus

9

What Do Polar Bears Do?

In winter, polar bears
sleep in a snow den.
Cubs are born
in the den.
In spring, the cubs
leave the den.

In summer, polar bears
hunt seals and walruses.

Seal

Walrus

13

They like to roll in the snow. They like to play fight. They like to sleep in the sun, too!

Index